GO ASK ALICE

New Women's Voices Series, No. 123

poems by

Liz Axelrod

Finishing Line Press
Georgetown, Kentucky

GO ASK ALICE

New Women's Voices Series, No. 123

ACKNOWLEDGMENTS

The author wishes to thank the following publications:

Night Terrors—*Counterpoint.com* (Sept 2014)
Another Full Moon Poem—*12th Street Journal* (Issue 4)
Collective Decay—*Ginosko Literary Journal* (Issue 14)
Slit Up to Here –*Ginosko Literary Journal* (Issue 14)
In Transit—*CounterPoint.com* (Sept 2014)
Music Box—*CounterPoint.com* (Sept 2014)
I'm My Own Worst Enemy—*12th Street Journal* (Issue 4)
Metaphysics Poem –*12th Street Journal* (Issue 3)
Daddy Dearest—Excerpt published in *Les Femmes Folles* (July 2014)
Photosynthesis—*Yespoetry.com* (Autumn 2013)
Quarry—*Yespoetry.com* (Autumn 2013)
Manhole Explosions—*Yespoetry.com* (Autumn 2013)
Shore Leave—*Nap.com* Log II
Blow Humpty—*Ginosko Literary Journal* (Issue 14)
The Book Everyone Says to Read—*Wicked Alice Zine* (December 2015)

Publisher: Leah Maines
Editor: Christen Kincaid
Cover Art and Design: Maxine Timm
Author Photo: Liz Axelrod

Printed in the USA on acid-free paper.
Order online: www.finishinglinepress.com
          also available on amazon.com

Author inquiries and mail orders:
Finishing Line Press
P. O. Box 1626
Georgetown, Kentucky 40324
U. S. A.

Table of Contents

CURIOSITY OFTEN LEADS TO TROUBLE

Photosynthesis 1

Collective Decay 2

Night Terrors.. 3

Metaphysics Poem 4

Slit Up to Here 5

In Transit 6

Why Can't I Be A Bird?... 7

GROWTH AND SHRINKAGE

Music Box.. 11

Another Full Moon Poem 13

I'm My Own Worst Enemy 14

Ancient Burial Ground... 15

Atmosphere.. 16

Quell.. 17

GARDEN OF CARDS AND THORNS

Quarry.. 21

Manhole Explosions... 22

Daddy Dearest 23

Shore Leave.. 25

Tossing Balls of Crumbled Waste Paper................................. 26

The Book Everyone Says To Read 27

Blow Humpty 28

CURIOSITY OFTEN LEADS
TO TROUBLE

Photosynthesis

"By-the-bye, what became of the baby?"
—Lewis Carroll, Alice in Wonderland

I thought leaves grew green 'cause you told me
they were made from sun and dirt and water

I thought grapes were purple 'cause you told me
they swapped color on the vine with leaves

I thought love was artificial like those Barbie dolls
you bought me when I asked what I would look like when I grew

How can anyone have a waist that small and hips so big
and how plastic must I be to learn to bend myself to Barbie life

when Ken doesn't have an anatomical presence
and I just learned they want to outlaw hugs in Tennessee

hugs are gateway drugs to be discouraged and sex is evil
Of course, it's impossible if you try it with your Barbie body

You told me I would bloom like unfurling leaves and grapes
and now I spend my hours drinking them fermented

as payment for my anti-light dependant interactions
I thought growth required only sun and dirt and water

Collective Decay

"Lastly, she pictured to herself how this same little sister of hers would, in the after-time, be herself a grown woman; and how she would keep, through all her riper years"
—Lewis Carroll, Alice in Wonderland

Nature has a formula that tells us when it's time
Everything alive will eventually die

Every living thing is a pulse. We quicken, then we fade
She goes outside for a walk and smells the scent of woodsmoke

Someone must have been burning a door
Last year, the fireplace was just decorative

People are destroying
everything in a desperate effort to survive

Life is short for small creatures, longer in big ones
Elephant hearts beat slowly, hummingbird hearts beat fast

Under a cloud of austerity, real smoke clouds as well
This rule seems to govern all life

When the formula says "you're done"
The daisy and the maple tree obey

When the watch-fob says, "it's time,"
                              We call it a day

Night Terrors

"We're all mad here. I'm mad. You're mad"
—Lewis Carroll, Alice in Wonderland

For endless
India ink miles the sky
is nothing but kaleidoscopes
long exploded

We focus
our 35mm lens
Forever turning

Sun-powered paths twist through
fallen brush and well-raked topsoil

Swollen boulders long for sugar shots
for sweet pink budding edibles,
for disappearing vapors
        One bite makes you larger
        One bite makes you smaller

Feed me, buy me Google Glasses
Super-glue keeps our edges neat

This miracle of stars
            is just illusion

Metaphysics Poem

"I don't think..." then you shouldn't talk, said the Hatter."
—Lewis Carroll, Alice in Wonderland

Cohesive Theory has me
Reflecting on Relativism
Things are not of themselves
Myself, I lack synonymy—
Attachment
The world is not as it would seem
Locke thinks it's all in the senses
Kant wants to categorize
Hume—I just don't get him
Hegal gives me language and synopses
Quine tells me there is no analyticity
I want synchronicity
My beliefs form the world
My conceptual scheme is neither
Analytic meaning nor
Synthetic fact
I'm searching for the point of contact,
Trying to organize my desires
Into a new reality
                    Fact is
I still want you
As an object of experience

Slit Up to Here

> *"Once more the pig-baby was sneezing on the Duchess's knee,*
> *while plates and dishes crashed around it"*
> —Lewis Carroll, Alice in Wonderland

A prodigal rock star can only be made
from piles of gravel found lying on the side of parking

lots with white lights and empty bottles.
No. Anything is possible but I have learned

not to think on probably anymore.
My elbow has been numb since 2001 when it got stuck

in between the #1 train and Penn Station.
Every few months it picks up static charge from subway cars.

There's a whole website devoted to snowflakes.
It doesn't taste right unless you melt it with your tongue.

The newspaper allows me to be angry
I ball up my passions in black ink and wait for

Angelina Jolie's slick back red-lipped six-pack
or at least her leg, sticking straight out of that black gown

all over the internet—
        scaring honey from the bees.

In Transit

"Well that was the silliest tea party I ever went to! I am never going back there again!"
—Lewis Carroll, Alice in Wonderland

You're a beautiful woman
said the drunken construction
consultant at Tracks,
the Penn Station watering-hole
with swivel chairs and sweet bartenders
who ease the pain of missing
that train by just one minute.

Let's keep in touch.
He didn't tell me his name
or text me his number.

Crazy bug-orange full moon!
Why don't I live in the city anymore?
Suburbs suck passion and bleach marrow.

I'm *Moonstruck.*
Hey! Did you know my biorhythms
and Nick Cage's are
a ninety-eight percent match?
Someone let him know, please.

What?
You don't believe in Astrology?
Blow me   (no really)   Blow me.

Lonely
Suffering full moon fever
from my kitten heels to the hoops
on my ears to the glass shards
of my
iced nipples.

Orange is calming and prevails
over fast food joints and train stations.

Why Can't I Be A Bird?

"What do you know about this business?' the King said to Alice
'Nothing,' said Alice."
—Lewis Carroll, Alice in Wonderland

This fleeting energy
wants to betray me

wants me to nest in verdant trees
red wings flapping wide.

I float on drone interpretations—
microburst in altitude adjustment.

This daylight's drawn in charcoal smudges
and wind-sheer mostly makes me nauseous.

Want to nest with me in verdant trees
red wings flapping wide?

I'm thinking
that it might be time
                          to flee

the swaying branches and meet
the present tense.

GROWTH AND SHRINKAGE

Music Box

> *"Never imagine yourself not to be otherwise than what it*
> *might appear to others that what you were or might have been..."*
> —Lewis Carroll, Alice in Wonderland

I am a collection
of well groomed follicles
and hand-colored
sound-bytes

Need some lube
and diamond files

I'm making movies
posing sexual
with strobe lights

I sit, stand, bend
while tough jocks
grind out emerald
painted cliffhangers

Cinema is fucking
with my psyche

I want pencil skirts
and cupid bangs,
sugar sticks
and cherry polish

Focus unconditional

I am not misty
I am not stunned
I am not wind-up

I am not my reflection

I am the Ballerina
on the box

leg outstretched
in hope of turning.

Another Full Moon Poem

"Who am I, then? Tell me that first, and then, if I like being that
person, I'll come up."
—Lewis Carroll, Alice in Wonderland

What if ownership of feeling
belonged solely
to the whims
of gravitational pull?

Stupid Moon!
You're nothing but a mannequin—
a pretty, pearly oyster shell.

Lead me round in circles
while my doctor writes
a paper cure.
No matter if it makes me
drive in my sleep,
no matter if it
removes synchronicity.

Why place gems in my path?
Why sit fat lighting the night sky
leaving only spikes
and bombs buried in the dirt

Waiting for the right foot
                    to set them off?

I'm My Own Worst Enemy

"Poor Alice! It was as much as she could do, lying down on one side..."
—Lewis Carroll, Alice in Wonderland

In another life I must have been
a goading crazy Monk
Whipping my back to shreds
Crying tears of blood and lust
Flailing at love's injustice

You see me as Goddess
Diana on the hunt
I see me as fallen
Arrow piercing flesh

Use your tongue   soothe
Appease my sorrow prayer
tear apart the silk
Mount my damaged disaster
be my master

Tortured torment
defeated wide and broken
I want your hands, your mouth,
your shuttering cock
Let me secure the ring
lash me with its salted sting

Kneeling in repose
awakening to mastery
Begging prostrate

Beating myself senseless
Calling empyrean Angels from ashes
naked lupine vellicate
devouring delicious wait

Ancient Burial Ground

"The executioner's argument was that you couldn't cut off
something's head unless there was a trunk to sever it from."
—Lewis Carroll, Alice in Wonderland

We blazed from room to room as if
running the labyrinth at Knossos

Taking Thesius' challenge
in the Minoan Palace

we slayed the Minotaur

Our attenuated bodies
bored through flesh and bone

Perfect proportions meeting
Praxiteles standards

Glazing, burning heathens

The wet spot drying
Sheets thrown to the wind

Phidian proportions be dammed
and you in my mouth

petrified as the waters evaporate

Your eyes travel centuries
turn to chiseled stone—

Constantine, guarding the Basilica
No blood moon illuminations

Only dust and aging

Atmosphere

"If I had a world of my own, everything would be nonsense."
—Lewis Carroll, Alice in Wonderland

Painting sky frames
on the bed
we spread open.

I lift my legs
while Saturn births
a hexagon cloud

Your hands slip
round the tight mist
of my tenderness

We rotate knowing
muscle always brings
our matter home

Quell

"How cheerfully he seems to grin, how neatly spread his claws,
and welcome little fishes in with gently smiling jaws!"
—Lewis Carroll, Alice in Wonderland

When waves take back their lapping waters,
when our chest no longer heaves
at chance   encounters

when the once filled hourglass drops
its last grains of sand
do we bury our desire on the beach and
hope for lightning strike   and crystallization?

The monthly pill ebbs and flows
some moons full to bursting
other moons bring heavy
drips   days and days   on end

Does blood crave salted water?

Crush >< Crash = miswired connections

I put the positive charge in the wrong socket
burned   my   fingertips   black

the steady flow   is done
now trite
now boring
these tears   have lost   their salt.

GARDEN OF CARDS AND THORNS

Quarry

"Curtseying as you're falling through the air! Do you think you could manage it? And what an ignorant little girl"
—Lewis Carroll, Alice in Wonderland

She can blink both eyes alternatively
but she can't eat gluten

Peanut butter sticks to her
dimples and causes unsightly bumps

on rice cakes and crumbles scratch
waste on her submarine hips

She tries to lay flat and smooth truth
out of her pasted lines and pebbles

She purports to describe the experience—
With pen and a few more loose-leaf sheets

she'll craft a pile large enough to stave
off paper cuts and wipe the blood

from last night's dive
into the glass cloud highway quarry—

All turquoise sheen and tractor trucks
unloading piles of useless pastel gravel

Manhole Explosions

"Down, down, down. There was nothing else to do..."
—Lewis Carroll, Alice in Wonderland

A girl I know
won $200K
from NYC
when one
broke her ankle.
It's getting harder
to walk up
Subway steps.
My legs take
on cement
and all the messy
cardboard homes
and body odor.
The same man
asks for dollars
on the corner
every day.
His collar veils
his scruff and
blown up face.
We walk by
grateful
for his frown
and blessing.

Daddy Dearest

"It's no use going back to yesterday, because I was a different person then."
—Lewis Carroll, Alice in Wonderland

Picture this for a moment
a page that truly heals

found on the internet at 2:30 a.m.
with all the tools and fixes

you would ever need to overcome
failings, longings, mistrust, jealousy;

and with unlimited healing powers
but only while you're watching Netflix.

I try to explain to my father
who is still stuck on age and violence

that there will be no more babies
but I'm quite certain

his Jello molds and candy
wrappers will remain sweetly tart

and satisfying, while rare beef
tempts me during all the separate

phases of the waxing moon.
You don't call anymore...

No. I've found a savior at
My Karma's Okay Dot Com.

I troll with myself and sort through
his selfishness, and why I have no desire

to pour sticky gel into that
particular fish-shaped copper mold.

The truth is, Daddy's lost his power
and the magnetic pull only affects

the soles of my feet when I'm
barefoot on the beach, in salt,

or searching online for polished stones
to fill the blue mason jars on my windowsill.

Shore Leave

"If you drink much from a bottle marked 'poison' it is certain to disagree with you sooner or later."
—Lewis Carroll, Alice in Wonderland

Electric pulse turns
sand to glass.
Salt erodes the
break-line.
Our unchecked
heat devours
clean white sand
now spotted
with refuse—
needles, condoms,
plastic bags,
blackened oily shells.
I gave you depth.
You dredged up garbage.
Storms give weight to water.
While crests lap up
this silent coast
pulling in upon
                    its shelf.

Tossing Balls of Crumbled Waste Paper

"Alice came to a fork in the road. 'Which road do I take?'
—Lewis Carroll, Alice in Wonderland

Today there has been too much talk of packing
binders into boxes, more so that we've begun tirelessly
viewing our sidewalks; as if to climb up would be to fall.

We kiss languorously and roll our tongues in sweet weather
avoiding handholds while locking fingers in empty space.

Sparkle and pop go the Dogwoods as they prove
bloom is the only way to exist. A man in white coveralls
is painting pastel walls while broken yards absorb his green.

Daunting task, this box-on-box mess, files of seasons
and molded folders desiring their place at the table.

There's always someone eating cold sesame noodles, never
enough soy. Soon large men will walk the halls and begin the
breakdown of the furniture. So much can slip through
the cracks, even with excel spreadsheets

folded into swans, but the Dogwood only blooms pink
for a moment, pointing its tight fists
at oncoming pick-up trucks.

The Book Everyone Says To Read

"You would have to be half mad to dream me up."
—Lewis Carroll, Alice in Wonderland

Hunger, hunter, husband, lover
left her picking up the bottom

of the fence to crawl and shoot a bow
and arrow at a deer one who doesn't answer.

Assemble all the children in the square.
Ask them to draw circles round and round.

Ask them to die for the crowds
then run on home as darkness falls.

Sky's the limit if you've got good aim.
You can shoot the shit out of this clown circus.

Today has me wishing for a less crowded car,
a bull-horn and no more wireless connections.

I don't have the strength to decipher your codes.
I read the Hunger Games in four hours.

Now I'm wondering what to do with my longbow finger,
why I suddenly feel the need to be shiny and satin blown

in order to stretch my plastic politics under piles of pillows,
between dog-eared penciled pages lost.

My screen is dark   and what the fuck
is that low-pitched buzzing   in the background?

Blow Humpty

"Alice knew it was the Rabbit coming to look for her, and she trembled till she shook the house, quite forgetting that she was now about a thousand times as large as the Rabbit"
—*Lewis Carroll, Alice in Wonderland*

Chick-A-Fil-A draws crowds and cheers
by refusing to serve my fine gay friends

They can go suck an egg.
It came before the chicken, anyway

And what rules do you new masters of republic require
to keep me firmly in my place

I'm barefoot and wondering what became of the freedoms
I never had to fight for in my childhood

Skirt length, pirouettes and math tests
replaced by gangs of hungry misanthrope and body armor

Like Humpty on the dessert wall
all cracked and leaking yellow with no water

Then Joshua comes and blows his horn and you tell me
I can't show my cleavage anymore

You mean to say, there's something other than *Legitimate Rape*
and my lady-parts protect me from unwanted pregnancy

Or maybe there's a baby waiting in the evidence
like honey sprouting from a bad seed

No. Those things just ferment

Yes, Chicken Little, the sky is falling
Is it sunstroke or mass marketing machines

building walls and flying drones
bombing ash and circumstance

and pockets full of posies rolling over
man flowing robes and man burning girls

We all fall down

Liz Axelrod is Poet, Adjunct English Professor, Book Reviewer, Social Justice Activist, and Grants Manager. She received her MFA from The New School in 2013. Her daughter, Maxine Timm, in her junior year of art school, is the cover artist for *Go Ask Alice*.

In her formative years Liz was a wild kid who made a career out of the party life. She was a late night DJ, spinning from 2:00am to 6:00am on her college radio station. But as we know well, late nights and parties don't make for good grades. So after spending seven years in three universities without earning a degree, she gave up at 26 and moved to NYC. After a short stint spinning records at clubs like Danceteria, The Limelight, Voodoo Lounge and The Surf Club, she tried out a slightly more stable life in the Music Industry. A few years and a couple of Gold Records later, she retired, married, moved to the suburbs, and had a baby.

However, the need to complete the college degree was a constant as she matured and looked at the world with a much clearer head and keener vision.

After her marriage ended in the late 2000's, Liz went back to college. Maxine was entering her freshman year of high school and already her path was in the arts. Liz knew she had to find her own path and set a good example for her daughter.

Liz's love of language was kindled and nurtured at The New School where she finished her undergraduate degree and went on to get her MFA in Creative Writing. She and her daughter would often do homework together and share their collective learning experiences. They both graduated with honors.

Liz also got doubly lucky in The New School's MFA program—it was there she met her fiancé, James Olson. Today they are both happily pursuing careers in Academia.

Being a single mom, working full time during the day and taking classes at night opened Liz's eyes. It also opened her mind, and after falling through her own personal looking glass, she has emerged with clarity, purpose and voice. There's much to be said about the pills that make you larger and the pills that make you small.

Go Ask Alice incorporates Liz's love of music and verse with her passion for language. The *Alice In Wonderland* epigraphs are in harmony with the poems, like background music. The book title comes from a song by Jefferson Starship that she often chose to end the evening with when DJing at the clubs. The cover art is Maxine's version of her mom's passion for poetry and their shared love of all things *Wonderland*.

CPSIA information can be obtained
at www.ICGtesting.com
Printed in the USA
LVHW111624070220
646226LV00002B/406